Denver

NUGGETS

BY K.C. KELLEY

Published by The Child's World®
1980 Lookout Drive • Mankato, MN 56003-1705
800-599-READ • www.childsworld.com

ISBN 9781503824706
LCCN 2018964188

Printed in the United States of America
PA02416

ABOUT THE AUTHOR

K.C. Kelley is a huge sports fan who has
written more than 150 books for kids.
He has written about football, basketball,
soccer, and even auto racing! He lives in
Santa Barbara, California.

TABLE OF CONTENTS

GO, NUGGETS!

The Denver Nuggets get their name from gold. **Miners** search for valuable nuggets of gold in the Colorado mountains. The Nuggets search for golden trophies! They have not won the NBA championship yet, but their fans keep cheering. Good young players have Denver ready to strike gold! Let's meet the Nuggets!

Nuggets rookie Torrey Craig flies high for a huge dunk.

Denver star Nikola Jokic uses his size and strength to hold off an opponent.

WHO ARE THE NUGGETS?

The Denver Nuggets are one of 30 NBA teams. The Nuggets play in the Northwest Division of the Western Conference. The other Northwest Division teams are the Minnesota Timberwolves, the Oklahoma City Thunder, the Portland Trail Blazers, and the Utah Jazz. The Nuggets have tough battles with their Northwest Division **rivals**!

WHERE
THEY CAME FROM

The Nuggets were one of the first teams in the American Basketball Association (ABA). That league started in 1967. Denver made the playoffs each year in the ABA. In 1976, some ABA teams moved to the NBA. The Nuggets made that big move! Since joining the NBA, Denver has not made the **NBA Finals** yet.

Check out the striped ball used by the Nuggets during their ABA days. Denver battled the Nets in this game.

9

Paul Millsap takes a shot in a game against Boston from the Eastern Conference.

The Nuggets play 82 games each season. They play 41 games at home and 41 on the road. The Nuggets play four games against each of the other Northwest Division teams. They play 36 games against other Western Conference teams. The Nuggets also play each of the teams in the Eastern Conference twice. That's a lot of basketball! In June, the winners of the Western and Eastern Conferences play each other in the NBA Finals.

The Nuggets' home court is in the Pepsi Center. The arena opened in 1999. The building is big enough to have a second court just for practice. The Nuggets share the Pepsi Center with other teams. The Colorado Avalanche pro hockey team plays there. The Colorado Mammoth plays pro lacrosse in the Pepsi Center. Fans pack the Pepsi Center for concerts by famous artists, too.

The Nuggets play in the Pepsi Center in Denver, where fans get help from Rocky, the team's mascot (left).

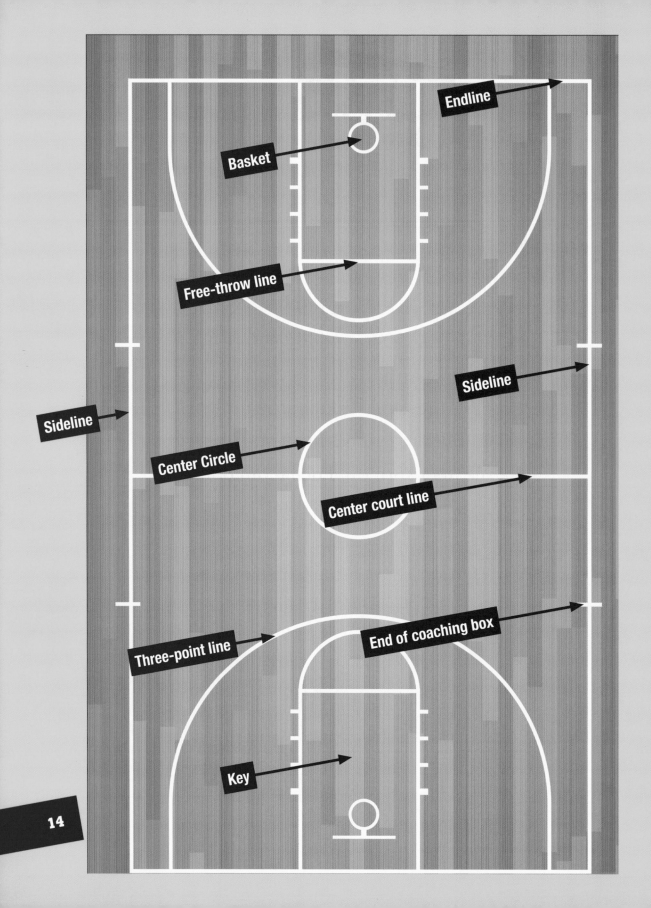

Endline

Basket

Free-throw line

Sideline

Sideline

Center Circle

Center court line

Three-point line

End of coaching box

Key

THE BASKETBALL COURT

An NBA court is 94 feet long and 50 feet wide (28.6 m by 15.24 m). Nearly all the courts are made from hard maple wood. Rubber mats under the wood help make the floor springy. Each team paints the court with its logo and colors. Lines on the court show the players where to take shots. The diagram on the left shows the important parts of the NBA court.

Here's a fun fact: The wood court at the Pepsi Center weighs 41,625 pounds (18,881 kg). The court is made with 233 separate pieces of wood. They fit together like a jigsaw puzzle.

GOOD TIMES

The Nuggets were one of the top teams in the ABA. They made the playoffs every season from 1967 through 1976. In the NBA, the Nuggets had a great 2008-09 season. They won the Northwest Division and made it to the Western Conference finals. They lost there to the Los Angeles Lakers, but it was a great season!

Denver's Dahntay Jones powers toward the basket during the 2009 Western Conference finals.

Denver's Tom Hammonds tried to grab this rebound in 1997. It slipped out of his hands. Denver did that a lot in a long, tough season.

TOUGH TIMES

The Nuggets' worst season came back in 1997–98. They lost a team-record 71 games! That is tied for the third most losses in an NBA season. What was the team's worst loss? In a 1980 game, the Nuggets fell to the Milwaukee Bucks by 48 points! In recent seasons, the team has struggled, too. The Nuggets did not make the playoffs from 2013-2018.

ALL THE
RIGHT MOVES

David "Skywalker" Thompson played seven seasons for Denver. He was famous for his slam dunks. He got his nickname for his leaping ability. Thompson soared above opponents to slam the ball into the net. Hall of Famer big man Dikembe Mutombo started his career with Denver. He was an expert at blocking shots.

In basketball, a "big man" means a player who is tall and strong. It can also refer to a team's best player.

Denver center Dikembe Mutombo was one of the best shot-blockers in NBA history.

Alex English played 10 seasons of his Hall of Fame career in Denver.

Dan Issel joined the Nuggets in 1975. He was one of the team's top scorers for the next 10 seasons. Alex English was an eight-time All-Star with Denver. He led the NBA in scoring in the 1982–83 season. Carmelo Anthony was another top scorer. He began his career with Denver in 2003 before moving to other NBA teams.

Most tall players are not great passers. Denver **center** Nikola Jokic is seven feet (2.13 m) tall but makes a lot of **assists**. He is the only NBA center with 15 assists in a game since 1970. Jokic grew up in Serbia. He makes many passes to **guard** Jamal Murray. This young player is a great shooter. Veteran Paul Millsap adds scoring skills, too.

25

Nikola Jokic became one of the top players in the NBA during the 2018–19 season.

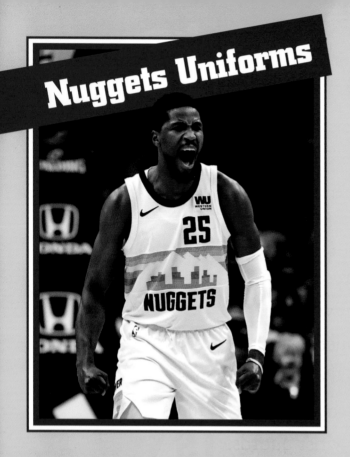

NBA players wear a **tank top** jersey. Players wear team shorts. Each player can choose his own sneakers. Some players also wear knee pads or wrist guards.

Each NBA team has more than one jersey style. The pictures at left show some of the Nuggets' jerseys.

The NBA basketball (left) is 29.5 inches around. It is covered with leather. The leather has small bumps called pebbles.

The pebbles on a basketball help players grip it.

TEAM STATS

H ere are some of the all-time career records for the Denver Nuggets. These stats are complete through all of the 2018–19 NBA regular season.

GAMES	
Alex English	837
Dan Issel	802

POINTS PER GAME	
Alex English	25.9
Allen Iverson	25.6

ASSISTS PER GAME	
Nick Van Exel	8.4
Fat Lever	7.5

REBOUNDS PER GAME	
Dikembe Mutombo	12.3
Julius Keye	11.2

STEALS PER GAME	
Fat Lever	2.5
Warren Jabali	2.1

FREE-THROW PCT.	
Mahmoud Abdul-Rauf	.916
Chauney Billups	.912

DAN ISSEL

29

SHORT
45

WARRIORS

POINTS	
Alex English	21,645
Dan Issel	16,589

GLOSSARY

assists *(uh-SISTS)* passes that lead directly to a basket

center *(SEN-ter)* a basketball position that plays near the basket

guard *(GARD)* a player in basketball who usually dribbles and makes passes

miners *(MY-nerz)* people who work in mines, digging for rocks and minerals

NBA Finals *(NBA FINE-ulz)* the championship series for the NBA

rivals *(RY-vuhlz)* two people or groups competing for the same thing

tank top *(TANK TOP)* a style of shirt that has straps over the shoulders and no sleeves

IN THE LIBRARY

Schaller, Bob and Dave Harnish. *The Everything Kids' Basketball Book (3rd Edition).* New York, NY: Adams Media, 2017.

Sports Illustrated Kids (editors). Big Book of Who: Basketball. New York, NY: Sports Illustrated Kids, 2015.

Whiting, Jim. *The NBA: A History of Hoops: Denver Nuggets.* Mankato, MN: Creative Paperbacks, 2017.

ON THE WEB

Visit our website for links about the Denver Nuggets:
childsworld.com/links

Note to Parents, Teachers, and Librarians: We routinely verify our Web links to make sure they are safe and active sites. So encourage your readers to check them out!

INDEX